Sas,
I hope this brings
back some memories
for you.
Jen.

16/03/93

Produced by AA Publishing

Captions by Richard Cavendish

Filmset by Wyvern Typesetting Ltd, Bristol
Origination by Scantrans Pte Ltd, Singapore
Printed and bound by New Interlitho SpA, Italy

The contents of this publication are believed correct
at the time of printing. Nevertheless, the publishers
cannot accept responsibility for errors or omissions,
or for changes in details given.

A CIP catalogue record for this book is available
from the British Library.

Published by The Automobile Association, Fanum
House, Basing View, Basingstoke, Hampshire
RG21 2EA.

ISBN 0 7495 0152 9

Front cover: Top – *Oxford, from Boar's Hill –
'dreaming spires'.*
Main – *Sidmouth with the cliffs of Salcombe Regis.*
Back cover: *Outwood Windmill, Surrey, with miller
feeding birds.*
Title page (opposite): *Footpath and hedgerow,
near Crediton, Devon.*

AA

visions·of

ENGLAND

Visions of England encapsulates the infinite variety of scenery that makes this country so special. From medieval castles to neat village greens nestling in the folds of gently rolling hills, this collection of pictures, specially selected from the AA's picture library, captures all that is quintessentially English.

Above *Villages are the fundamental units of English rural life and a key ingredient of England's charm. At Castle Combe, in Wiltshire, smoke rising gently into the winter sky is all that moves in a characteristically tranquil scene of village houses with their church. In the background, at the top of the main street is the covered medieval market cross.*

Right *Mellow Cotswold limestone and thatch combine to create the allure of these cottages in the Gloucestershire village of Stanway. The use of local materials makes a village blend naturally into the surrounding landscape.*

Left *Thatched roofs again, but here a frame of stout timber beams has been filled in with brick, in the village of Brampton Bryan, in Hereford and Worcester, close to the Welsh border.*

England

Right *The traditional building material in Devon was cob, a mixture of clay, straw and dung, and walls were usually at least 3ft (1m) thick. Cottages are often whitewashed or colour-washed to weatherproof them. Thatch for the roof has the advantage of a lighter weight than stone or slate.*

8

Above *In the Middle Ages the cheapest and most readily available building material was wood. This late 15th-century half-timbered construction, perched crazily over the moat, is the gatehouse of the even older manor house at Lower Brockhampton in Herefordshire. The property is now looked after by the National Trust.*

England

Below *At Coln St Aldwyns, in Gloucestershire, the River Coln winds its gentle course through lush water meadows on its way to join the Thames. The village, whose church was originally dedicated to the obscure St Aldwyn, lies downstream from Coln St Dennis and Coln Rogers.*

Right *An almost impossibly quaint cottage at Minstead in the New Forest, in Hampshire. The walls of red brick are covered with creeper and the bedroom floor windows peep demurely out from under the thatch. Even the outhouse at the back has its own rustic thatched roof.*

Right *Decorative thatch on a house in Dulverton, in Somerset, on the southern edge of Exmoor. Many thatched roofs have an ornamental trim at points where reinforcement is needed, such as along the ridge.*

Left *An idyllic scene at Finchingfield in Essex, near Thaxted. With its village green, duckpond and whitewashed cottages, this is a particularly photogenic place. In the background, the church's squat Norman tower is crowned by an 18th-century cupola.*

Following spread *The Atlantic in gentle mood laps milkily at the rocks and creams over the sand at Bedruthan Steps, a celebrated beauty spot near Newquay, on the north coast of Cornwall. The massive rocks are supposed to have been used as stepping stones by the giant Bedruthan. Access to the beach is down a steep stair from the top of the cliffs.*

Above *The swirling water of the weir in the foreground sets off the statuesque elegance of Pulteney Bridge, crossing the Avon in Bath. Designed by Robert Adam, it was inspired by Florence's medieval shop-lined bridge, the Ponte Vecchio. The 18th-century development of Bath was a conscious attempt to bring back the grandeur of Imperial Rome.*

Right *The girl, the shop and the bicycle are all thinking pink in Trim Street, one of Bath's graceful 18th-century streets, which recall the days when fashionable society gathered there to take the healthful waters.*

Below *Bath Abbey is seen through the arch in York Street, which was constructed in the 19th century to recall the city's Roman heritage. The abbey dates principally from the 16th century and was the last important church built in England before the Reformation.*

Left *The Royal Crescent, completed in 1775, was the masterpiece of John Wood the Younger, junior member of the father-and-son pair of architects who designed 18th-century Bath. There are 30 houses in the terrace, which is more than 600ft (183m) long. It is seen here from the Royal Victoria Park.*

Opposite page *The quay and haven at Mousehole (pronounced 'Mowzel') on the southern coast of Cornwall. Once an important fishing port, it now makes its living primarily by tourism. England's long relationship with the sea has involved fishing, trade, exploration, defence and holidays.*

Above *Stately east coast sailing barges at Pin Mill, on the River Orwell in Suffolk, upstream from Harwich. Boats like these used to carry the coastal trade between London and the East Anglian ports.*

Right *Boats on the seafront at Sidmouth. This decorous resort on the South Devon coast was developed in the early 19th century to take advantage of the new fashion for sea bathing and seaside holidays.*

Right *In medieval times beacons were erected at hazardous points along the coast to warn ships, and from the 16th century permanent lighthouses were built. The hexagonal one at Godrevy Point, in a particularly dangerous area of the northern Cornish coast, dates from 1859.*

Below *Like most lighthouses today, the one at Hartland Point on the savage North Devon shore is no longer manned, but is operated automatically. The days when lighthouse keepers might be marooned for weeks by ferocious seas have passed.*

Right *The pointed chalk spikes called the Needles, which lie off the western end of the Isle of Wight, rise to a height of 100ft (30m). They were originally connected to the mainland by a chalk ridge, but this has been slowly eroded away. The red-and-white striped lighthouse was built in 1859.*

Left *At Southwold on the Suffolk shore, a North Sea fishing village and minor seaside resort, the lighthouse gleams white against a threatening sky. Resorts were being developed along the remote Suffolk coast by the mid-19th century.*

Left *The highest cliff on the south coast of England is Golden Cap, which looms 626ft (190m) above the English Channel and the Dorset shoreline near Lyme Regis. The need to protect beautiful stretches of the coast is increasingly recognized, and this area is owned and safeguarded by the National Trust.*

Above *Towering cliff bastions guard the North Yorkshire coast near Robin Hood's Bay. Much of this area, again, belongs to the National Trust and is also protected as part of the North York Moors National Park.*

Left *Demonstrations of their skills by craftsmen have become tourist attractions in the post-war years. This man is making dolls' houses at the Craft Village at Arreton on the Isle of Wight.*

Left *The blacksmith at work in his forge at the Powder Mills at Postbridge in Devon. After 1945 traditional crafts seemed to be in danger of dying out altogether as victims of the industrial revolution and the machine age. Recent years and growing affluence, however, have seen them revive.*

Left *At the village of Kilburn, North Yorkshire, the main attraction is the wood-carving workshop which continues the tradition of the late Robert Thompson (he died in 1955). His work, which can be found in many churches, carries his signature of a mouse — sometimes in intriguingly covert locations.*

Right *Spinning by hand at the Yorkshire Museum of Farming in Murton, near York. In the past spinning was so much a part of everyday domestic life that unmarried girls were called 'spinsters'.*

23

England

Right *Hardraw Force, near the village of Hardraw in the Yorkshire Dales, is the highest single drop waterfall in England, falling some 90ft (28m) down a limestone cliff. A path leads behind the fall, from which you can look out through the water. 'Force' is a North Country word for a waterfall, originally from a Norse word.*

Left *In the Cornish beauty spot of St Nectan's Glen, close to Tintagel, a waterfall drops 40ft (12m) into a basin or 'kieve', in which, according to tradition, the saint was buried. St Nectan was a Dark Age missionary who came from Wales to bring Christianity to Cornwall and Devon.*

Right *The upper falls on the River Ure at Aysgarth in Wensleydale, which is the only one of the Yorkshire Dales not named after the river that runs through it. The falls are attractively set among woods by an old mill.*

England

Opposite page *England's rich heritage of houses and interiors covers the whole scale from the grandiose to the comparatively humble. The superbly elegant interiors of the saloon and the dining room in Saltram House in Devon were designed by Robert Adam in the 1770s. The house, near Plymouth, is owned by the National Trust.*

Right *Anne Hathaway's Cottage at Shottery, just outside Stratford-upon-Avon in Warwickshire, is a half-timbered Elizabethan farmhouse which was the birthplace of Shakespeare's wife. It is one of the attractions which make Stratford the most visited town in England outside London.*

Right *Preparing a meal in costume in the kitchen of the house in Cockermouth, Cumbria, where William Wordsworth was born in 1770, and his dearly loved sister Dorothy a year later. The house now belongs to the National Trust.*

England

Previous spread
Mompesson House in the graceful cathedral close in Salisbury, Wiltshire, was built at the turn of the 17th and 18th centuries by a wealthy Salisbury family. The interiors, notable for their sumptuous plasterwork, date from about 1740. It is now owned by the National Trust.

Opposite page *The English genius for gardening is amply demonstrated in the series of romantically beautiful 'garden rooms' created at Scotney Castle, near Tunbridge Wells in Kent, by successive generations of the Hussey family, and now cared for by the National Trust. The ruins of the 14th-century castle lend enchantment to the views.*

Above *Romantic seclusion in Sussex: at Goring-by-Sea on the West Sussex coast near Worthing, Highdown Gardens were created in an old chalkpit.*

Near right *A trim for the topiary on the terrace at Bowood, the Earl of Shelburne's stately seat near Calne, in Wiltshire. The house is surrounded by one of the most stunningly beautiful parks in England, landscaped by Capability Brown in the 18th century, and there is a separate rhododendron garden covering 50 acres.*

Left *A Norman hold in the Welsh Marches, worn by time and weather, stands quietly in the snow on a winter morning. Snodhill Castle is near Dorstone, in Hereford and Worcester. The ruined fortress, on a steep motte, or artificial mound, was built in about 1200.*

Below *Grimly menacing, but not the real thing: Eastnor Castle, near Ledbury in Hereford and Worcester, is an early 19th-century imitation of a Norman castle. It was built for the first Earl Somers by Sir Robert Smirke, and work began on it in 1812.*

33

England

Below *Farm carts in another fine barn, in Glastonbury, built in the 14th century for Glastonbury Abbey and now home to the Somerset Rural Life Museum. The barn is noted for its collar-beam roof, in which the tie-beam is high up the roof slope.*

Right *As farming methods have changed almost out of recognition since World War II, rural museums have sprung up to preserve the implements and atmosphere of the agricultural past. These waggons at Wimpole Hall in Cambridgeshire are in the Home Farm's magnificent barn, which was designed by no less an architect than Sir John Soane.*

DRAINING
THE
LAND

THE
ESTATE

Far left *Farm machinery, a millstone and an assortment of nostalgic enamel advertising signs make a rustic still life from the days of the horse to the age of the car at a countryside collection at Winkleigh, near Hatherleigh in central Devon.*

Left *Carts locking horns in the rural museum at Calbourne Mill, near Newport on the Isle of Wight. The watermill here is in working order and visitors can see it in operation in the summer.*

Right *Floodlit in majesty above the gleaming Thames, Tower Bridge has become a symbol of London for many visitors, though the decline of London as a port means that the weighty leaves of the central drawbridge no longer rise as often to let ships through as they did in the 1890s, when the bridge was completed.*

37

Left *A squadron of the Life Guards jingles along the Mall in its finery of scarlet and steel. The senior regiment in the British Army, the Life Guards trace their history back to the Commonwealth period in the 17th century, when the future Charles II was living in exile in Holland and a personal escort of exiled Cavaliers was formed to protect him.*

Above *Another potent symbol of London is Big Ben, the 316ft (96m) clock tower of the Houses of Parliament. The huge cracked bell which tolls the hours stands 7ft (2m) high and weighs close to 14 tons. Each of the minute hands on the four clock faces travels a total of 25 miles (40km) every year. The present Westminster Bridge, on the right, was built in 1862, three years after Big Ben was completed.*

England

Left *Looking upstream along the Thames from Tower Bridge to London Bridge, with Southwark Bridge just beyond. The top of the dome of St Paul's can be seen on the right. Moored in the river on the left is* HMS Belfast, *a World War II cruiser which took part in the D-Day landings of 1944 and is now a floating naval museum.*

Above *Golden and gleaming, the winged Victory stands atop the white marble Queen Victoria Memorial in front of Buckingham Palace. Unveiled in 1911, the monument was designed by Sir Aston Webb and the sculpture is by Sir Thomas Brock. The queen herself is majestically seated at one side, with groups of figures representing Justice, Motherhood and Truth on the others.*

England

Right *Ennerdale Water in the western part of the Lake District, under an ominous sky with the high fells looming in the background. The lake, which lies in the course of the River Liza (known as the River Ehen as it flows out to sea), is a reservoir and its water level has been raised by an unobtrusive dam.*

Left *Ullswater is the second largest of the Lake District's lakes (only Windermere is bigger). This curving stretch of water, 7¹/₂ miles (12km) long, is often claimed as the most beautiful lake in an area famed for the most magnificent scenery in England. The great bulk of Helvellyn towers up to the south-west and Place Fell is near the southern tip.*

Right *The steam yacht* Lady of the Lake *plies on Ullswater, with wonderful views of the surrounding mountain scenery. The Lake District was scooped out by Ice Age glaciers and when the ice finally melted, lakes were left in the hollows.*

Left *There are no really high mountains in England, but there are some impressive peaks all the same. Ingleborough, 2373ft (723m), is one of the limestone summits of the Pennine Chain, a magnet for fell walkers in the Yorkshire Dales National Park. It is seen here from the north-west, near Chapel le Dale.*

Above *The jagged and tumbled quartzite rocks of the Stiperstones, south-west of Shrewsbury, are in the Shropshire Hills official Area of Outstanding Natural Beauty. The highest point is 1759ft (536m). Lead was mined here in the past. The ridge has a sinister look and the outcrops have such names as The Devil's Chair and Nipstone.*

Left *Saddleback, or Blencathra, rising to 2847ft (868m) in Cumbria north-east of Keswick, is made of Skiddaw slate, which is geologically the oldest type of rock in the Lake District, laid down some 400 million years ago.*

Right *A lock at Berk-hamsted in Hertfordshire on the Grand Union Canal, which runs from London to Birmingham. Rivers had always been an important means of transporting goods, people and news in England, but the Canal Age at the turn of the 18th and 19th centuries brought a new era of swift and efficient water communications. Canals were soon overtaken, however, by the even newer and swifter railway network.*

Above *Since 1945 the river and canal system has enjoyed a fresh lease of life as a pleasure and holiday boating network. One of the most popular canals is the Shropshire Union, which connects Birmingham with the Manchester Ship Canal at Ellesmere Port. This flight of locks is at Audlem in Cheshire.*

Left *A narrowboat on the River Thames near Eaton Hastings in Oxfordshire. The whole culture of 'canal art', brightly painted canal boats and their lavishly decorated equipment, adds to the interest of pleasure boating. The yards where narrowboats were built had their own individual emblems and styles of decoration.*

Left *A Wallis and Steevens traction engine gets an overhaul, or a 'pull-through', at the Alscott Farm Agricultural Museum in Shebbear, North Devon. The application of steam power to agriculture during the 19th century was an early challenge to the dominion of the horse, well before the advent of the internal combustion engine.*

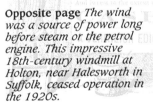

Opposite page *The wind was a source of power long before steam or the petrol engine. This impressive 18th-century windmill at Holton, near Halesworth in Suffolk, ceased operation in the 1920s.*

47

Right *Local bygones on show in the Preston Hall Museum, at Stockton-on-Tees in Cleveland, include enamel advertising signs of the kind familiar earlier in this century on the sides of houses and shops, and at railway stations.*

Left *Steam power has vanished from British Rail's lines, but preservation societies and enthusiastic amateurs have made sure that it has not vanished altogether. Here a steam train on the North Yorkshire Moors Railway runs through lonely Newtondale on part of its scenic journey between Pickering and Esk Dale in the North York Moors National Park.*

Above *One of the engines on the Lakeside and Haverthwaite Railway in Cumbria. This line's trains connect with the steamers on Lake Windermere and run through wooded country from the southern end of the lake to Newby Bridge and Haverthwaite, a few miles to the south.*

Left *Coupling up, on the Lakeside and Haverthwaite Railway, which owns steam and diesel locomotives. A whole generation which never knew the Age of Steam has been introduced to it by the preserved railways.*

Right *Cathedrals ancient and modern: the Roman Catholic cathedral of Christ the King in Liverpool was designed by Sir Frederick Gibberd in a highly modernistic style in the 1960s. The vast circular nave surrounds a central altar which is a 19-ton block of white marble.*

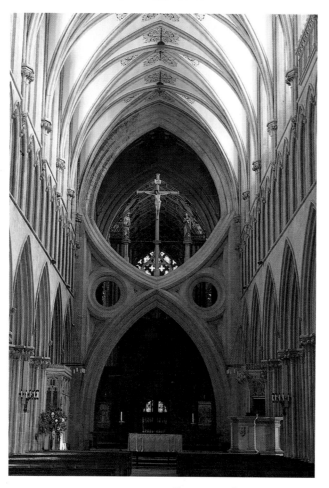

Above *Another remarkable, but much older cathedral interior is the one at Wells in Somerset, where huge double 'scissor' arches, like a pair of nutcrackers, were erected in the 14th century to help take the weight of the tower. On the western arch is the rood, or crucifix, flanked by figures of the Virgin Mary and St John.*

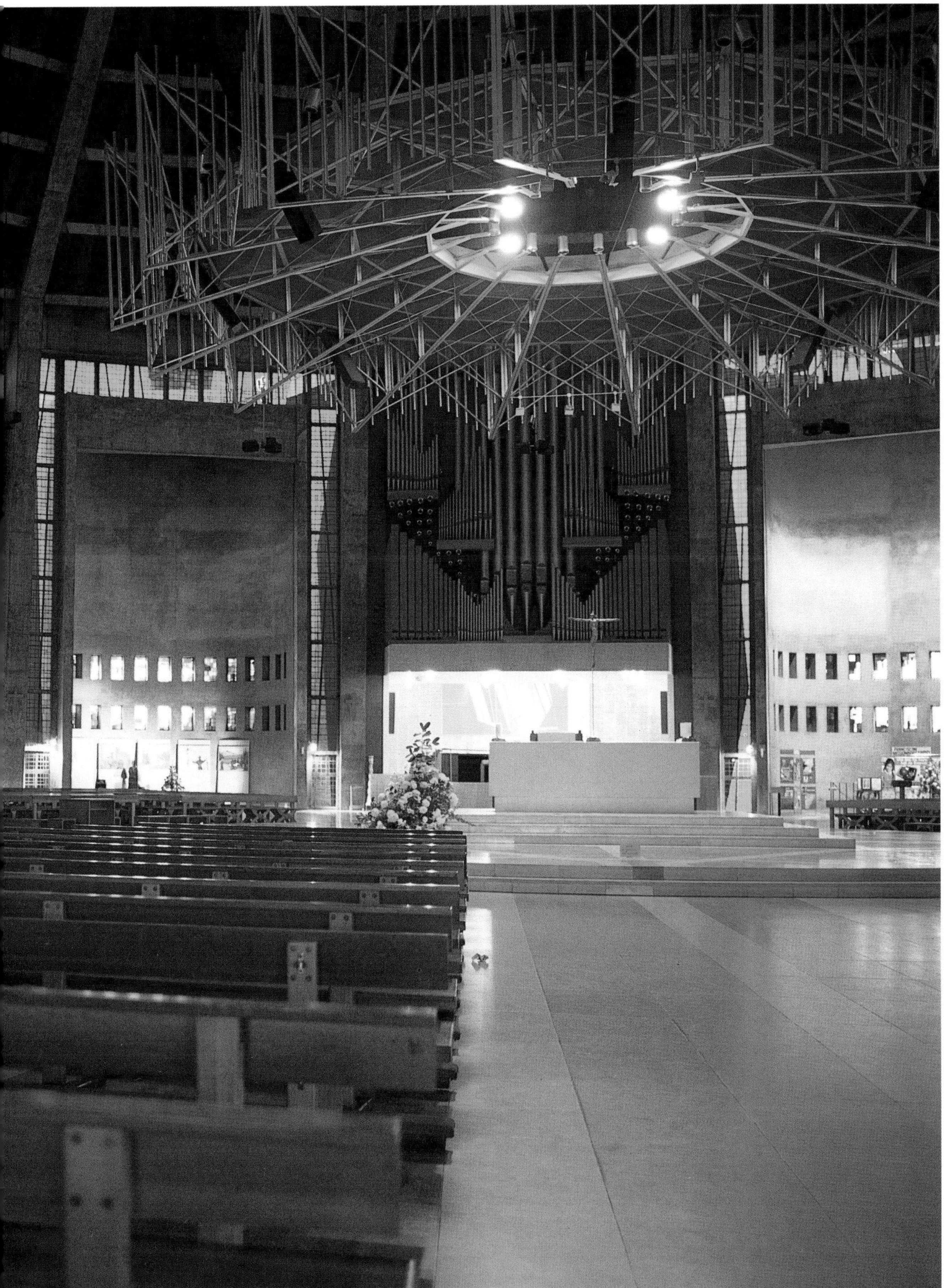

Right *The most spectacularly situated of all English cathedrals is Durham, rearing up on its high wooded rock in a horseshoe bend of the River Wear. Building began in 1093 on the site of an older Saxon church, enclosing the shrine of St Cuthbert, the most revered saint of the North of England. The cathedral today is a magnificiently impressive Norman edifice.*

Left *Seen from the medieval city walls is York Minster, one of the largest churches in Europe and the cathedral of the archdiocese of York. The church, which is specially famous for its stained glass, has recently been repaired after the latest in a long series of catastrophic fires.*

Above *View along the chancel of Peterborough Cathedral, looking towards the altar, with the mirror giving a view of the roof. This is another Norman cathedral, begun in 1117 to replace the Saxon church. Queen Katherine of Aragon, first wife of Henry VIII, was buried in the cathedral and the body of Mary, Queen of Scots was interred here for 25 years after her execution.*

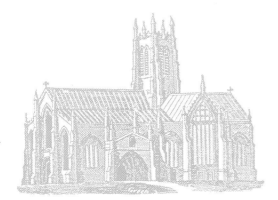

Right *Long before the Romans conquered England, prehistoric men left their mark on the landscape. On a ridge overlooking Herefordshire's tranquil Golden Valley is Arthur's Stone, a Stone Age tomb whose original covering mound of earth has worn away over the centuries. The giant capstone is 18ft (5½m) long. Many monuments and landmarks were named after King Arthur, the great legendary ruler of Britain.*

Below *A close-up view of the head, eyebrows and round goggling eyes of the Cerne Abbas Giant. This strikingly virile, club-carrying figure, 180ft (55m) tall, is carved on the side of Trundle Hill, above Cerne Abbas in Dorset. Who he is and why he is there, no one really knows.*

Above *Rising enigmatic and eerie from the low-lying ground close to the River Brue, Glastonbury Tor in Somerset was probably a sacred place long before Christianity came to Britain. In legend it is closely linked with King Arthur and with the Holy Grail. The tower on top is all that is left of the medieval church of St Michael.*

Right *In Cornwall the 'quoits' are Stone Age tombs whose earth covering has worn away. This one, Trethevy Quoit, stands on Bodmin Moor, north of Liskeard. The tilted capstone is over 11ft (3m) long and the tallest supporting stones are close to 15ft (4¹/₂m) high.*

Left *This large and totally mysterious object is Silbury Hill, near Avebury in Wiltshire. It is not a natural hill at all, but a man-made mound, about 130ft (40m) high, covering more than 5 acres. Archaeological investigation has found no indication that anyone was buried in it and no evidence of what it was for.*

England

Below *Stonehenge in Wiltshire, the most famous prehistoric monument in Britain, was constructed and altered over many centuries. The huge upright stones weighing 20 to 30 tons each were dragged across country for 20 miles (32km) or more and erected with the aid of ramps. The lintels were fitted across the top with mortise-and-tenon joints. The whole complex represents an immensely impressive feat of organization and engineering in a society without modern machinery.*

Right *The avenue of standing stones which leads to the stone circles at Avebury in Wiltshire. Small markers indicate the positions of stones no longer in place. This was probably a processional way used by priests and attendants at the major religious festivals of the year.*

Left *The Castlerigg stone circle, also known as the Keswick Carles, in a beautiful setting in the Lake District near Keswick. This may be one of the oldest stone circles in Britain, and its seems clear that it was used as an astronomical observatory as well as a religious site.*

59

Right *The Robbers' Bridge, south-east of Oare, on Exmoor. Now protected as a National Park from damaging development, Exmoor is delightful walking and riding country, with red deer, wild ponies and a wealth of animal and bird life.*

Left *Badgworthy Water runs through the peaceful Doone Valley, along the Devon–Somerset border on Exmoor. Beyond the tree is a memorial stone to R D Blackmore, whose romantic novel* Lorna Doone *still brings many visitors to explore the countryside in which it is set. Blackmore based his story on local traditions of a gang of robbers who kept the whole district in a grip of fear in the 17th century.*

Right *Crossing the River Barle on Exmoor is Tarr Steps, north-west of Dulverton in Somerset. This primitive bridge of stone slabs has often been washed away by floods and rebuilt, as happened after the severe flood of 1952, when it is said that 9 inches (23cm) of rain fell on the moor in 24 hours.*

Index

The page numbers in this index refer to the captions and not necessarily to the pictures accompanying them.

Acknowledgements

All the photographs in this publication are from The Automobile Association's photo library, with contributions from:

M Adelman, A W Besley, P & G Bowater, R Czaja, P Davies, S King, A Lawson, S & O Mathews, E Meacher, R Newton, R Rainford, B Smith, R Surman, M Trelawny, H Williams, T Woodcock and J Wyand.